World War I

Lisa Zamosky

Publishing Credits

Historical Consultant
Jeff Burke, M.Ed.

Editors
Wendy Conklin, M.A.
Torrey Maloof

Editorial Director
Emily R. Smith, M.A.Ed.

Editor-in-Chief
Sharon Coan, M.S.Ed.

Creative Director
Lee Aucoin

Illustration Manager
Timothy J. Bradley

Publisher
Rachelle Cracchiolo, M.S.Ed.

Teacher Created Materials
5301 Oceanus Drive
Huntington Beach, CA 92649-1030
http://www.tcmpub.com

ISBN 978-0-7439-0664-7

Table of Contents

World War I—The "Great War" 4–5

The Spark That Started the War 6–7

Choosing Sides 8–9

The Early Battles 10–11

The War Widens 12–13

America Moves Closer to War 14–15

A Famous Note 16–17

The Home Front 18–19

Aces in the Sky 20–21

The Russian Revolution 22–23

The Central Powers Almost Won 24–25

Casualties and Blame 26–27

What World War I Means Today 28–29

Glossary 30

Index 31

Image Credits 32

World War I—The "Great War"

In 1914, a war began in Europe. People living back then called it the Great War. More nations battled in this war than in any other war before it. It lasted from 1914–1918. A total of 65 million soldiers fought in this war. More than 19 million people died around the world. It is one of the largest human **catastrophes** (kuh-TASS-truh-feez) in world history. Today, this war is called World War I.

British troops charge German lines near Tower Bridge in France.

The problems that caused this war had been brewing for quite some time. Some countries were becoming very rich. As a result, they wanted to expand their land. These countries in Europe had big armies and navies. But, they still needed support when they tried to take land from other countries. This produced jealousy and conflicts among the nations.

Building Up Forces

By 1914, Germany had more than eight million soldiers in its army. Russia had four million soldiers, and France had three million soldiers. Great Britain built up its navy. In fact, the British navy was almost as big as all of the other navies combined.

One Embarrassing Event

In 1870, France was in a battle with Germany but lost. So, Germany took over two French **provinces** (PRAW-vuhnts-ez). The French felt very embarrassed by this loss. It gave the French a reason to fight against Germany.

Did You Know?

The assassination of Archduke Ferdinand was the second attempt on his life that day. Earlier in the day, a bomb was thrown at his car. He blocked it with his arm. It bounced away and damaged the car behind the archduke's car. People in that car were hurt by the blast.

A Blank Check

Germany quickly took sides with Austria-Hungary. Germany promised to help them in any way they needed. Some historians say this was like giving Austria-Hungary a blank check. This gave Austria-Hungary the confidence to declare war on Serbia.

An American Nurse Stays to Help

Mary Borden was traveling through Europe in 1914 when the war broke out. Instead of returning home, she stayed and helped. Borden set up and ran a hospital unit to help wounded soldiers. She was awarded a medal by the French government for her bravery and hard work.

EUROPE 1914

The Spark That Started the War

Serbia (SIR-be-uh), Greece, and Bosnia (BAHZ-nee-uh) were countries that had one thing in common. They had fought for independence from the Turkish Ottoman Empire. But freedom did not last long for Bosnia. Bosnia is located in between Serbia and Austria-Hungary. Unfortunately, these two larger countries did not get along.

Many Austrians were afraid that Serbia would attack Austria-Hungary. So, the Austrian army moved into Bosnia. There,

Bosnia had an unlucky location. It was stuck between two feuding countries.

Archduke Ferdinand and Sophie were shot on their way to a hospital. They wanted to visit the men who were injured in the assassination attempt that took place earlier that day.

they set up protection from Serbia. Bosnians did not like this at all. Bosnia was not a free country anymore. Many Serbians agreed with Bosnia that it was wrong.

The future king of Austria-Hungary was named Archduke Francis Ferdinand. He and his wife, Sophie, traveled to Bosnia. While there, a Bosnian **assassinated** (uh-SAS-uh-nate-uhd) both of them. However, this Bosnian lived in Serbia. So, Austria-Hungary leaders blamed Serbia for these murders. They put unreasonable demands on Serbia. The leaders of Serbia felt badly about the murders, but the country could do nothing about it. In just one month's time, Austria-Hungary declared war on Serbia.

Choosing Sides

Some of the powerful nations in Europe built up military forces. Then, they joined the war. The Germans wanted to go to war against both France and Russia. Germans believed they could easily defeat France. However, they worried about facing the huge Russian army. The Russians planned to attack eastern Germany.

Great Britain tried to remain **neutral**. As long as Germany did not attack France, the British would not join the war. On August 3, 1914, the Germans declared war on France. The German troops moved into Belgium the next day. France was at risk. Great Britain was determined to stop Germany. So, the British entered the war.

By the middle of August 1914, the two sides in Europe were clear. There were two great **alliances** (uh-LYE-uhntz-ez). Germany and Austria-Hungary were on one side. They were known as the Central powers. On the other side were Great Britain, France, and Russia. Together these countries were known as the Allied forces, or the Allies.

Cheering soldiers are eager to head to France and help fight against the German forces. A difficult journey awaits these young men.

More Join In

Japan and Italy joined the Allied forces shortly after the war began. Turkey entered the war and joined the Central powers.

Americans Fight with Canadians

President Woodrow Wilson wanted to keep the United States out of the war. However, 60,000 Americans volunteered to join Canadian troops as part of the British forces in the war.

A Woman Joins the Ranks

Flora Sandes was a British nurse who wanted to help fight in the war. The Serbian army let her join as a soldier. Before long, Sandes was promoted to sergeant major. She was wounded during the war but remained in the army. When she retired, she was a captain.

German soldiers prepare for battle from the trenches.

The Early Battles

In the first weeks of the war, the German army was strong. It defeated both French and British forces in Belgium. But by the next month, the German forces were tired and losing strength. This is when the Battle of the Marne took place in France. This battle lasted for seven long days. French forces stopped the Germans and made them turn around.

Trench Warfare

Long ago, enemies faced each other on flat battlefields. By the early 1900s, that no longer happened. The German soldiers dug the first **trenches** of the war. A typical trench was about 10 feet (3 meters) deep. This protected soldiers from enemy fire.

Deadly Battles

Some very deadly battles were fought in this war. The Germans launched an attack against the French in a battle near Verdun (vuhr-DUHN), France. An estimated one million soldiers died or were wounded.

German troops defeat the Russians at the Battle of Tannenberg. The battle lasted for five days in August 1914.

The Russian army **mobilized** (MOH-buh-lized) quickly. It invaded eastern Germany and won the Battle of Gumbinnen (goom-BIN-nen) on August 20, 1914. More Russians attacked Germany from the south. The Germans had to quickly move troops to protect themselves.

Russian troops did not win all their battles, though. At Tannenberg (TAN-uhn-burg), the Russian army lost 125,000 men. Two weeks later, Germans killed 100,000 more Russian troops. Later battles between these two armies were more evenly matched.

The War Widens

New **front lines** opened across Europe. The country of Turkey tried to attack Allied forces on the Suez Canal in Egypt. Turkey's attack failed. This area was important to Great Britain. It was a transportation link to the British colonies in India and the Far East.

On April 25, 1915, the British, Australian, New Zealand, and French troops joined together. They landed on a long strip of land called the Gallipoli (guhl-LIP-uh-lee) peninsula. This was located in Turkey. The Battle of Gallipoli turned into a very long trench

Troops land on the rugged terrain of the Gallipoli peninsula. They encountered strong ocean currents, steep cliffs, wide gullies, and heavy enemy fire.

British troops march through the thick bush in East Africa.

battle. It was very hot in the summer and bitterly cold in the winter. The weather created terrible conditions for the troops. By January 1916, the Allied forces had withdrawn. More than 250,000 Allied soldiers had died there.

The war was not going well for the Allies. It seemed like Germany was unstoppable. German troops attacked Serbia. They pushed Russians out of Poland and the three **Baltic States**. It was going so well that the Germans began planning a huge German empire in eastern Europe.

Africa and China in the War, Too?

Allied troops attacked German colonies in Africa. Later, Japan captured a German-controlled **port** city in China. They did this with the help of British and Indian troops.

Deserting the Army

The Russian army was successful in a number of battles against Austrian and German troops. But millions of Russian soldiers were killed or wounded. This was too much for some Russians to bear. Russian soldiers began deserting the army in large numbers.

The Sinking of the *Lusitania*

On May 1, 1915, the *Lusitania* (loo-suh-TAY-nee-uh), a British ocean liner, set sail from New York City. A few days later, a German submarine torpedoed the *Lusitania*, sinking the ship and killing 1,198 passengers. Americans were very angry, but the United States still did not enter the war.

U-boats

German submarines were called U-boats. This is an abbreviation for the German word *unterseeboot*, or undersea boat.

This German U-boat was put on display in New York. U-boats like this one sank enemy ships by firing underwater torpedoes.

The *Lusitania* only took 18 minutes to sink. It sank off the coast of Ireland.

America Moves Closer to War

President Woodrow Wilson did not want to take sides in Europe's war. Instead, he hoped that the United States could help to bring a peaceful end to the war.

In February 1915, Germany announced that it considered the waters around Great Britain to be a war zone. Many of the boats there carried **munitions** (myoo-NIH-shunz) to Great Britain. These materials helped Great Britain fight the war. The German government declared that it would attack all boats in those waters. This included U.S. ships, too. This was called unrestricted submarine warfare. It made President Wilson angry. Germany backed down from its threat because it did not want to bring America into the war.

In January 1917, Germany changed its mind. They began using unrestricted submarine warfare. They thought it was the only way to win the war. At that time, President Wilson broke off official talks with Germany.

A Famous Note

For a long time, the United States tried to remain **impartial** (im-PAR-shuhl). However, in early 1917 the United States learned some new information. The Germans sent a coded telegram to Mexico. It was called the Zimmermann telegram because a German official named Arthur Zimmermann wrote it. In it, Germany encouraged Mexico to join the Central powers. The Germans believed they would own the United States after the war. So, they promised to give Mexico land from the United States after the war. When people in the United States found out about Germany's plan, they were very upset. The United States entered the war and joined the Allies.

The Allies were glad to have the United States on their side. Before that, it seemed as though the war would never end. General John Pershing led the first American unit to France and Belgium. His **battalion** (buh-TAL-yuhn) of soldiers paraded in Paris. The soldiers were young and not ready for war. Even so, they were welcomed as heroes by thousands of French citizens.

On April 2, 1917, President Wilson asked Congress for a declaration of war. Four days later, America declared war on Germany.

The Zimmermann telegram was intercepted by the British. They decoded it and showed it to the Americans.

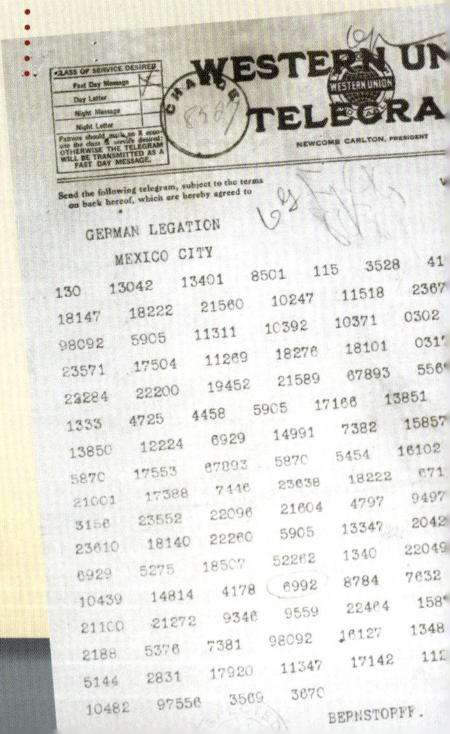

CLASS OF SERVICE DESIRED
Fast Day Message
Day Letter
Night Message
Night Letter
Patrons should mark an X opposite the class of service desired; OTHERWISE THE TELEGRAM WILL BE TRANSMITTED AS A FAST DAY MESSAGE.

WESTERN UN
TELEGRA
NEWCOMB CARLTON, PRESIDENT

Send the following telegram, subject to the terms on back hereof, which are hereby agreed to

GERMAN LEGATION
MEXICO CITY

130 13042 13401 8501 115 3528 41
18147 18222 21560 10247 11518 2367
98092 5905 11311 10392 10371 0302
23571 17504 11269 18276 18101 031
22284 22200 19452 21589 67893 556
1333 4725 4458 5905 17166 13851
13850 12224 6929 14991 7382 15857
5870 17553 67893 5870 5454 16102
21001 17388 7446 23638 18222 671
3156 23552 22096 21604 4797 9497
23610 18140 22260 5905 13347 2042
6929 5275 18507 52262 1340 22049
10439 14814 4178 6992 8784 7632
21100 21272 9346 9559 22464 158
2188 5376 7381 98092 16127 1348
5144 2831 17920 11347 17142 112
10482 97556 3569 3670

BEPNSTOPFF.

The League of Nations

President Wilson made a speech to the nation about building peace after the war. He spoke about freedom of the seas and reducing weapons. He spoke of the right of nations to rule themselves. He also talked about building the League of Nations. He believed the League of Nations could help countries resolve differences and avoid going to war.

Pershing's Past

Before World War I, Pershing spent time fighting the Plains Indians. He also fought in the Spanish-American War. He led a special cavalry unit for part of that time. His unit was made up of African Americans. That was very rare for the 1800s.

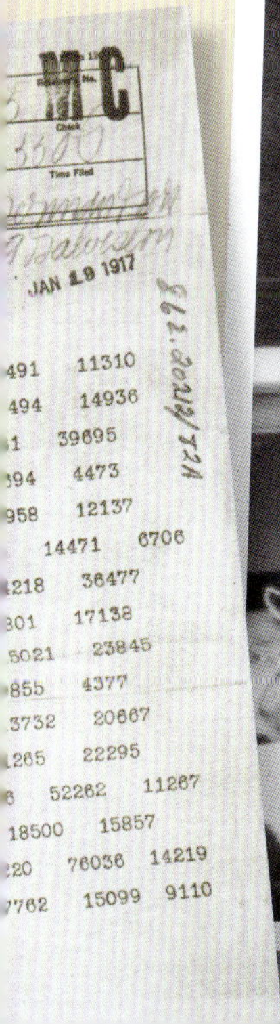

General Pershing prepares to go to war. When Pershing returned home from the war, he wrote a book about his experiences.

The Home Front

President Wilson needed all Americans to support the war. To do this, he created the Committee on Public Information. This committee used the media to spread anti-German **propaganda** (prah-puh-GAN-duh). They hoped this propaganda would increase support for the war.

For the most part, this plan worked. Orchestras refused to play symphonies by German composers. Citizens all over the United States burned books that were written in German. In some towns, no one was allowed to speak German. Entire communities came together to support the war. Boys went off to fight with pride and joy. Twenty-four million men registered for the draft. More than six million were sent into service.

Not everyone supported the war, however. Some men tried to avoid service. These men were called **draft dodgers**. The U.S. government employed thousands of volunteers to hunt down the draft dodgers. And, more than 65,000 Americans refused to fight in the war for religious reasons.

Writing About the War

Elizabeth Shepley Sergeant was a journalist. She traveled all the way to the front lines. She wrote reports for the *New Republic* newspaper. Sergeant was seriously injured during the war. After the war, she wrote a book about what she saw. The book was titled *Shadow Shapes: The Journal of a Wounded Woman*.

Liberty Bonds

President Wilson knew that the war would be very expensive. He decided to raise money to help pay for the war through the sale of liberty bonds. Liberty bonds could be cashed in for their original value plus interest.

This poster was printed in 1914. It shows Mother Russia standing over the leaders of Germany and Austria-Hungary.

Even children helped fund the war effort. They could buy war savings stamps for a quarter. If the children collected enough stamps, they could trade them in for liberty bonds.

Aces in the Sky

Just a few years before the war, Wilbur and Orville Wright had made the first manned flight. During the next few years, airplanes changed a lot. Flying during World War I was very dangerous. At first, war planes were used for spying on the enemy. Soon, planes with machine guns in front of the pilots were used. These planes shot down enemy planes. At times, a gun's bullets hit its own plane's propeller and caused the plane to crash. The Germans invented a gun that stopped when the propeller moved in front of it.

Before long, Germany used bomber planes. Some of the German bombers were able to carry bombs weighing as much as 660 pounds (299 kg). One time, German bombers dropped 72 bombs in the heart of London. The planes used by the British could not fly high enough to reach the bombers. Thus, the Germans did not lose one bomber plane during this attack.

The Allied forces began to develop their own air power. Great Britain had begun the war with 63 airplanes. By the end of the war, the country had 22,000 aircraft. Great Britain emerged from World War I as the strongest air power in the world.

To be considered an "ace," a pilot had to bring down five enemy aircrafts. This was a slightly easier task if you were flying this plane, a Sopwith F1 Camel.

American Eddie Rickenbacker not only flew fast in his airplanes, he also drove fast in his cars. He was a racecar driver before he became a fighter pilot.

Learning to Fly

Katherine Stinson was the fourth woman in the world to receive a pilot's license. She taught her daughter, Marjorie, and son Eddie, how to fly. Together, the family trained many of the fighter pilots that flew in the war.

What's a Sopwith Camel?

The Sopwith F1 Camel became the most successful Allied fighter plane. It made shooting down German aircraft easier. This plane was able to make very sharp turns at high speeds. Pilots liked to fly this plane because it was very easy to fly.

The Russian Revolution

While Russian troops were fighting in World War I, the Russian **citizens** were unhappy. They did not like life under the rule of **Czar** (ZAR) Nicholas II. The Russians had just lost a war with Japan in 1905. Their armies were not prepared for another war. So many soldiers died that the czar forced farmers to take their places. When the farmers left, no one could plow the fields. People began to starve. Upset Russians rioted in the streets of the capital city. Some soldiers even joined the crowd.

A man named Vladimir Lenin (VLAH-duh-mir LEH-nuhn) wanted things to change in his country. He supported **communism** (KAWM-yuh-nih-zuhm). This means that the government controls the lives of everyone. In 1917, he led citizens in the Russian Revolution. He took control of the government. When Lenin came into power, he withdrew Russian forces from the war. Lenin organized the country into several self-governing sections. These sections formed the Union of Soviet Socialist Republics, or USSR.

Protestors march through St. Petersburg during the Russian Revolution in 1917.

Lenin's Revenge

When Lenin was 17, his brother, Alexander, was hanged for plotting to kill the czar. This tragedy caused Lenin to deeply hate Russia under the rule of czars.

Lenin Returns

Lenin's ideas were not popular with the czar's government. So, Lenin was arrested and sent into **exile** (EK-sile). In 1917, the Germans arranged for Lenin to return to Russia. They believed that Lenin and his supporters would create unrest in Russia. This unrest would turn Russians against the war. That would give Germany an advantage in the war.

This painting shows rebels attacking Russian leaders at the Winter Palace. This was during the Russian Revolution.

The Central Powers Almost Won

At the beginning of 1918, it looked like the Central powers would win the war. Russia was out of the war. Large numbers of United States troops had not arrived in France yet. And, German troops were close to capturing Paris, France's capital city.

But German troops were getting weaker. There were not enough supplies. The men were getting hungry. There were strikes and

Men and women celebrate in the streets of New York City. Germany has surrendered.

Happy American soldiers dance with women in the streets of France.

Meeting in Versailles

In 1918, the German government sent a letter to President Wilson. It asked for a **truce** and peace talks. President Wilson went to the peace talks, which were held in Versailles (vuhr-SI), France. On June 28, 1919, the Treaty of Versailles was finally signed.

Girl Power

Over 13,000 women enlisted in the navy and marines during World War I. Most were nurses or "Hello Girls." Hello Girls were bilingual switchboard operators. These women spoke two languages and helped relay information between important people during the war.

mutinies (MYOO-tuh-neez) among German soldiers. Germany's railroad network was falling apart. Food and other important supplies were running low.

By November 1918, Germany asked to discuss peace with the Allies. After more than four years of war, German soldiers **surrendered** (suh-REN-duhrd). On November 11, 1918, Germany signed an **armistice** (ARE-muhs-tuhs) agreement. Cries of joy were heard throughout the world. French, British, and American soldiers paraded through the streets of Paris. In London, women and children danced in the streets.

Everything Changes

Across the world, the war changed everything. Large countries were broken up. New, smaller states were set up. Czechoslovakia (chek-uh-slow-VAW-kee-uh) and Yugoslavia (yoo-go-SLAH-vee-uh) were two of these new states. German colonies in Africa and Asia came under British or Japanese control. The world was a different place after 1918.

Adolf Hitler

The Allies had no idea that a German named Adolf Hitler was watching them. Within the next 20 years, he would rise to power in Germany. He gained support by speaking out against the World War I treaty. Germans felt it was very unfair to them.

This British trench was captured by the Germans. Living in trenches was not easy.

Casualties and Blame

Historians can only estimate the total number of soldiers killed in World War I. Many soldiers died because of the terrible conditions in the trenches. Wounded soldiers were sometimes left there to die alone. Men who were not rescued often bled to death. Some wounded soldiers were captured and killed by the enemy. As the war continued, governments stopped reporting how many men were killed. The high numbers made citizens want to give up fighting in the war.

The Allies won the war. So, they decided the terms of the peace treaty. Germany had to give up its colonies. The Allies forced Germany to end its air force and its navy. The treaty allowed Germany to keep an army of only 100,000 men. The war cost the Allies a lot of money. So, they expected Germany to pay them back. This was a heavy burden for Germany. The Germans complained. However, the Allies forced the Germans to accept all the blame for the war. Some people felt this was not fair.

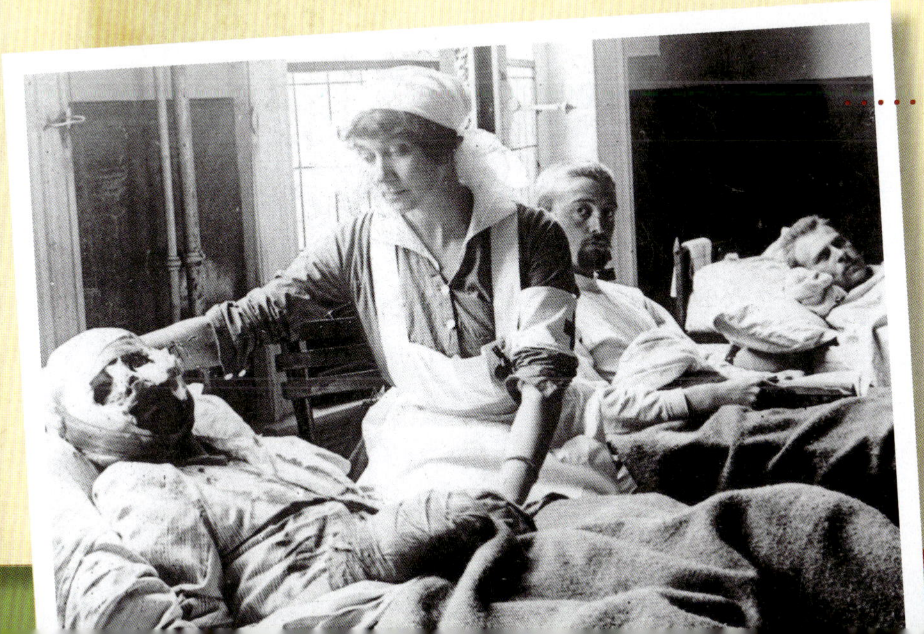

A nurse tends to a badly wounded soldier. Hundreds of thousands of soldiers were injured during the war.

What World War I Means Today

To understand the world today, people must look back at the beginning of World War I. Many problems in the Middle East come from that time. The British defeated the Turks, whose land was in the Middle East. After the war, people agreed that the Jewish people needed a homeland of their own. They talked about giving them land in Palestine (PAL-uhs-tine). It took 20 years, but this was the first step in creating Israel (IZ-ree-uhl). Today, the Israelis (iz-RAY-leez) and Palestinians (pal-uhs-TIN-ee-uhnz) fight over this land. The British also drew borders that still separate groups of people around Iraq. Today, these groups still fight one another.

The soldiers who fought in World War I thought they were fighting a war that would end all wars. They thought it would never be forgotten because it was so important. However, people today do not

Soldiers parade through the streets of Minneapolis after returning home from the war.

know much about this war. It is sometimes called the Forgotten War. There are no big national monuments to honor the men who fought. Even so, the effects of this war still impact life today. And, World War I set the stage for the next big war, World War II.

This map shows how the world changed after World War I.

The Nobel Peace Prize of 1919

President Woodrow Wilson was given the Nobel Peace Prize in 1919. The prize was awarded for his work to establish the League of Nations and the Treaty of Versailles.

A World Power

The United States did not want to be in this war. And yet, the country came out of the war as a world power.

Glossary

alliances—close associations of nations or other groups

armistice—a temporary end of fighting through agreement among parties; a truce

assassinated—murdered by surprise attack; usually a prominent person for political reasons

Baltic States—three countries along the Baltic Sea: Lithuania (lih-thuh-WAY-nee-uh), Latvia (LAT-vee-uh), and Estonia (eh-STO-nee-uh)

battalion—a large group of organized troops

catastrophes—tragedies or disasters that harm many people

citizens—people who live in a country

communism—an economic policy where the government distributes all land and goods equally to the people

czar—ruler or emperor of Russia long ago

draft dodgers—men who are drafted for the army but instead run away from that duty

exile—forced absence from a homeland

front lines—the areas of direct contact between opposing combat forces

impartial—treating or affecting all equally

mobilized—assembled, prepared, or put into operation

munitions—weapons including bullets, guns and gun powder for making bombs

mutinies—times when people rebel against their leaders

neutral—not aligned with, supporting, or favoring either side in a war, dispute, or contest

port—a place on a waterway with facilities for loading and unloading ships

propaganda—material passed out by people with a certain viewpoint that tries to convince others of that same viewpoint

provinces—territories governed as administrative or political units of countries or empires

surrendered—to give up or give in; to not win

trenches—deep furrows or ditches

truce—a temporary end of fighting by agreement of the opposing sides of a war; an armistice

Index

Africa, 13, 26
African Americans, 17
Allied forces, 8–9, 12–13, 20
Allies, 8, 13, 16, 25–27
Asia, 26
Austria-Hungary, 6–8, 19
Baltic States, 13
Battle of Gallipoli, 12–13
Battle of Gumbinnen, 11
Battle of Marne, 10
Battle of Tannenberg, 11
Belgium, 8, 10, 16
Borden, Mary, 6
Bosnia, 6–7
Central powers, 8–9, 16, 24
China, 13
communism, 22
Congress, 16
Czechoslovakia, 26
Egypt, 12
Europe, 4–6, 8, 12–13, 15
Ferdinand, Francis, 6–7
Ferdinand, Sophie, 7
France, 4–5, 8–10, 16, 24–25
Gallipoli peninsula, 12
Germany, 5–6, 8, 10, 13, 15–16, 19–20, 24–27
Great Britain, 5, 8, 15, 20
Greece, 6
Hitler, Adolf, 26
India, 12
Iraq, 28
Ireland, 14
Israel, 28
Italy, 9
Japan, 9, 13
League of Nations, 17, 29
Lenin, Alexander, 23
Lenin, Vladimir, 22–23
Liberty bonds, 18–19
London, 20, 25
Lusitania, 14
Mexico, 16
Middle East, 28
New Republic, *The*, 18
New York City, 14, 24
New Zealand, 12
Nicholas II, 22
Nobel Peace Prize, 29
Palestine, 28
Paris, 16, 24
Pershing, John, 16–17
Poland, 13
Rickenbacker, Eddie, 21
Russia, 5, 8, 23–24
Russian Revolution, 22–23
Sandes, Flora, 9
saving stamps, 19
Serbia, 6–7, 13
Sergeant, Elizabeth Shepley, 18
Sopwith F1 Camel, 20–21
Spanish-American War, 17
Stinson, Eddie, 21
Stinson, Katherine, 21
Stinson, Marjorie, 21
St. Petersburg, 22
Suez Canal, 12
Tannenberg, 11
Tower Bridge, 4
Treaty of Versailles, 24, 29
Turkey, 9, 12
Turkish Ottoman Empire, 6
Wilson, Woodrow, 9, 15–18, 24, 29
Wright, Orville, 20
Wright, Wilbur, 20
U-boats, 14
Union of Soviet Socialist Republics (USSR), 22
United States, 9, 14, 16, 18, 29
Verdun, 10
Yugoslavia, 26
Zimmermann, Arthur, 16
Zimmermann telegram, 16
World War II, 29

Image Credits

cover Bettmann/Corbis; p.1 Bettmann/ Corbis; pp.4–5 The Granger Collection, New York; p.6 Teacher Created Materials; p.7 Bettmann/Corbis; pp.8–9 Corbis; p.10 The Granger Collection, New York; p.11 Popperfoto/Alamy; p.12 Bettmann/ Corbis; p.13 The Print Collector/Alamy; p.14 The Library of Congress; pp.14–15 Library of Congress; pp.16–17 (top) The Library of Congress; pp.16–17 (bottom) The National Archives; p.17 The Library of Congress; p.18 Library of Congress; pp.18–19 The Library of Congress; p.19 Library of Congress; pp.20–21 (top) Bettmann/Corbis; pp.20–21 (bottom) Bettmann/Corbis; p.22 Photos.com; p.23 Photos.com; p.24 Bettmann/Corbis; p.25 Bettmann/Corbis; p26 (left) Library of Congress; p.26 (right) The Library of Congress; p.27 The Granger Collection, New York; p.28 The Library of Congress; p.29 Teacher Created Materials